WAITING ON GOD'S TIMING ...
                    WITH GRACE

WAITING ON GOD'S TIMING ...
WITH GRACE

Rev. Dr. Myra K. Pritchett

Forewords by Rev. Gary L. Colter and
Rev. Dr. Margaret Watson

Powder Springs, GA

Waiting On God's Timing...With Grace
by Rev. Dr. Myra Pritchett

Published by J&C Legacy Publishing
www.jclegacypublishing.com

All rights reserved. This book or any portion thereof may not be reproduced or used in any manner whatsoever without the express written permsission of the publisher except for the use of brief quotations in a book review.

Unless otherwise noted, all Scripture quotations are from the New International Version, Zondervan Publishing House, Copyright © 1984

Scripture quotations marked KJV are from the King James Version, public domain.

Scripture quotations marked ESV are from the English Standard Version from The Holy Bible, Copyright © 2000, 2001 by Crossway Bibles, a division of Good News Publishers Used by permission. All rights reserved.

Cover design by Chanelle Watson
Author Photograph by Andrew Joseph

Copyright © 2022 by Myra Pritchett

Published in Powder Springs, Georgia
by J&C Legacy Publishing.

Printed in the United States of America

ISBN: 979-8-218-12003-0

In Loving Memory
of
Irving Woodrow Pritchett
and
Lillie Louise Pritchett

A Message from the Author

I humbly stand on the shoulders of many great pastors and leaders who have sown into my spiritual life.

"And we beseech you, brethren, to know them which labour among you, and are over you in the Lord, and admonish you; And to esteem them very highly in love for their work's sake. And be at peace among yourselves."
1 Thessalonians 5:12-13 KJV

My deepest appreciation and thanks to...

Reverend Gary L. & Lady Diane Colter
Reverend Dr. Margaret Watson
The late Dr. Otis Hugee II
The Late Bishop Allen McDaniel
Reverend Dr. Thomas Samuel Cooper Jr.
Mother Ruth Roseboro

Brother Andrew Joseph, Photographer
Sister Jada Joseph, Assistant
J&C Legacy Publishing, LLC

Foreword
By Rev. Gary L. Colter

Rev. Dr. Myra Pritchett, my daughter in the ministry, is a wonderful, powerful, preacher, teacher, and kind woman of God. Her ministry will transform the lives of many that are waiting for God to move.

While waiting on God, Myra has faced many personal challenges, but her willingness to trust God has developed her ministry. Without any sacrifices there will be no victory. Matthew 16:24 says,

"Whoever wants to be my disciple must deny themselves and take up their cross and follow me."

The sacrifices Myra has made to raise her boys and to take care of her mother, show her tenacity and stamina.

Rev. Dr. Myra Pritchett has blessed us at the Mount Lebanon Baptist Church with her knowledge of the Word of God, and her signature phrase, *"I am Single, but I am Saved"*.

I am so proud to be your Pastor and Lady Diane your First Lady. Just remember,

> "Time is filled with swift transition,
> None on earth unmoved can stand,
> Build your hopes on things eternal
> hold to God's unchanging hand."

It's about *holding* on to God's hand as you are waiting in ministry.

Much love from your Pastor,

Rev. Gary L. Colter
Mt. Lebanon Baptist Church
Peekskill, New York

Foreword
By Rev. Dr. Margaret Watson

The words declared by the prophet Isaiah in Isaiah 40:31, *"But they that wait upon the Lord shall renew their strength; they shall mount up with wings as eagles; they shall run, and not be weary; and they shall walk, and not faint,"* echo Myra Pritchett's life.

We met as teachers in the Board of Education in 1989. The Lord quickened my Spirit and said, *"Pray for her!"* I prayed for 6 years. I took my time, waited, and under the unction of God, I witnessed and introduced her to Jesus Christ.

Soon after, she began to attend church services, bible study and joined the Mt. Calvary Pentecostal Church in Yonkers, New York. I became her pastor and she, my spiritual daughter. Myra was taught, baptized in Jesus' Name, and filled with the Holy Ghost with tongues of fire.

God gifted her with *"divers kinds of tongues"*. As she spoke Hebrew, Arabic, Spanish, and Mandarin, He released to me the interpretation. Then, God gave me *"word of knowledge"* and said, *"Tell her to write."*

I witnessed her non-stop hunger for the Word of God. I immediately recognized not only her gift of writing, but her gift of teaching. In whatever capacity I asked her to serve, Myra did it willingly and with excellence. I watched her bring her children to church and she demonstrated agape love toward me, ALWAYS. Myra learned to walk in holiness as God began to elevate her.

Myra Pritchett, as an author, has been given this incredible topic, *Waiting on God's Timing...with Grace*. There is no better time for one to read this book. A book inspired and sanctioned by God to encourage the body of Christ. There were occasions when I read authors referencing "time," sadly their references or substance of time had been watered down. In *Waiting on God's Timing...with Grace*, Myra does an awesome job of thoroughly explaining the concepts of time.

I especially love how she started with

what time is from God's timeline versus man's timeline. She explains, *"time is broken down into two ancient Greek words called Chronos and Kairos"* and *"Chronos and Kairos don't run concurrently"*. I also love the way she then ties the breakdown of what time is to help us understand waiting and timing are intertwined. She declares, we all play the "waiting game".

There are 97 scriptures in the Bible that reference time. The Holy Bible speaks about man's thoughts. In Genesis 1:26-31, God made man in His own image and that took time. It took God 6 days to make man, which was God's Kairos time, where He spoke and it was so. That sealed it right there. Evolution had nothing to do with it. It was all in God's timing.

Waiting on God's timing is never easy. It can be challenging and compelling, causing impatience. Apostle Paul addressed the Roman church in Romans 5:3-6, and reminds us,

> *"we glory in tribulations also: knowing that tribulation worketh patience; And patience, experience; and experience,*

> *hope: And hope maketh not ashamed; because the love of God is shed abroad in our hearts by the Holy Ghost which is given unto us. For when we were yet without strength, in due time Christ died for the ungodly."*

I would always tell my spiritual daughter to wait on the Lord and get busy building the Kingdom of God. Down through the years I have watched her journey through years of seminary while raising her children. Myra has gained the experience, education, and obedience to God to become a humble servant by evangelizing while doing street ministry. This included feeding the homeless on the streets and shelters in Harlem, visiting nursing homes, and counselling the broken-hearted. Waiting on God is an ode to her life's testimony.

In her book she addresses, "How You Wait Matters". Myra *is an example* that "the wait" matters. When you learn how to wait because you are confident in whom you are waiting on, destiny is going to fulfill your timing. Time means to wait as in laboring. Discouragements may creep in to bring doubt, but your faith will make you whole and bring experience because you are growing into perfection.

> *"Therefore, my beloved brethren, be ye stedfast, unmovable, always abounding in the work of the Lord, forasmuch as ye know that your labour is not in vain in the Lord."*
> *1 Corinthians 15:58 KJV*

Dr. Rev. Margaret Watson, B.L.A, ThB, MSEd, PsyM., M.Ed, DMin.
Pastor, Mt. Calvary Pentecostal Church
Yonkers, New York

Table of Contents

A Message from the Author — ix
Foreword by Gary L. Colter — xi
Foreword by Rev. Dr. Margaret Watson — xiii
Preface — xxi

Chapter 1
The Difference Between God's Timing and Man's Timing
1

Chapter 2
The Necessity of Waiting on God's Timing
17

Chapter 3
Perspectives of Time
53

Chapter 4
Waiting Grace
61

Chapter 5
God is Waiting on Us; God Waits Too
73

Chapter 6
Waiting for the Blessing After the Promise
87

Chapter 7
The Assurance of God's Timing Coming to Pass
99

Chapter 8
The Timing of the Writing of This Book... Why Now?
107

Chapter 9
Waiting On God Is A Ministry Practical Application
110

Notes	117
Bibliography	119
Acknowledgements	121
About the Author	123

"But they that wait upon the LORD shall renew their strength; they shall mount up with wings as eagles; they shall run, and not be weary; and they shall walk, and not faint."

~Isaiah 40:31

Preface

A Lady in Waiting

Questioning God's timing is not a new phenomenon in and of itself. Questioning God about waiting on time, takes on a whole different light. I have always been intrigued, if not fascinated, by the multiple aspects of time such as, what time means to us and to God, as well as the definition of the components of time. In our basic science classes in school, we learned time is observable, factual, irreversible, eternal, sequential, and has measurable pockets of events.

Observable, in that time can be seen in the moment or over time. Factual, in that it is genuine and accurate. Irreversible, in that time is one directional. Eternal, in that it has always existed and has no beginning and no ending. Sequential, in that time is an ordered succession of moments. Measurable, in that time can be quantified in size, length, and amounts.

On the other hand, the Bible has its own voice when it comes to defining time, especially the "waiting parts". Throughout the Bible, God makes distinctions between His time, Kairos, and our time, Chronos. However, I could not completely understand, since God holds time in His hands, why He seemed to take so long moving time along! Why is He not in a hurry? Better yet, why am I in a hurry!

Perhaps, you too are wondering, how or where you fit into God's timetable. If you are contemplating this thought, you are in great company! One thing is certain and that is, we must accept His Divine timetable for every season or stage of our lives. Regardless of the various things that tend to separate man into little pockets of differences, we are all human with like natures. We have an innate need to satisfy our desires to know the times and the seasons that concern our lives.

The Word of God tells us about occasions where God's timing was immediate, like when He healed by His spoken Word. Then, God tells us about times of waiting, especially in the prophetic realm. The Lord has allowed me to witness His immediate miraculous healing of the lame and the born-again experience of a soul receiving the Gift of the Holy Spirit with the tongues of fire! I've heard several testimonies of believers who have also borne witness to God's immediate response to their prayers. Still, others waited for God's appointed time to experience their blessings and were delivered or made whole, while others sat in waiting. We serve an awesome God! So, why then do we still question and even complain about "the wait"?

My journey began many years ago and has brought me to this point of penning the words of this book. I wanted to write this book because I struggled with waiting on God's timing, like so many of us do. I often wanted to jump ahead of Him without considering what He thought, felt, or even what He wanted for me. I thought I knew what was best for me, more than God. I was reminded of two facts from the Word of God...

> *"it is hard to kick against the pricks."*
> *Acts 26:14g KJV*

> *"For my thoughts are not your thoughts, neither are your ways my ways, saith the Lord."*
> *Isaiah 55:8 KJV*

In a microwave, automatic, autonomous, self-driven world, we need to slow down, stop doing drive-bys, and come to a full stop. God is speaking! I asked myself, what was God thinking when He created us? He had been fellowshipping with Jesus and the Holy Spirit and yet, in due time, He decided to create a world. God placed man in it, with all the creations He needed to sustain himself yet, from the time of creation until now, it has been a time-centered world. Everything moves according to God's will, not ours.

During my training at seminary, I still

found myself in waiting. Seminary taught me many valuable things but it did not satisfy my need to have a Holy God explain why His timing and my timing never seemed to be in sync. I thank God that His mercy and grace have been great toward me. He put up with my impatience and stubbornness. I realize that as I waited on God's timing in my life, He was waiting on me too! What a divine revelation; that an awesome, Holy and magnificent God was waiting on me to catch up to His Perfect, Divine and Appointed Time!

As you wait on God's timing, let me offer up a prayer for you.

Heavenly Father,

Thank you for setting time in motion and for allowing us to be a part of it. Your love, steadfastness, and compassion toward us defy the limits of time. As we wait on your perfect and Divine will to come to pass, teach us how to wait on you in word, action, and deed, knowing that we are safe in the hollow of your hands.
In Jesus Name, Amen.
~ Myra P.

WAITING ON GOD'S TIMING ...
WITH GRACE

"But, beloved, be not ignorant of this one thing, that one day is with the Lord as a thousand years, and a thousand years as one day."

2 Peter 3:8 KJV

Chapter 1

The Difference Between God's Time and Man's Time

> "What happened to the years gone by; drifting silently down the paths of passing moments. All I see is what I saw. What I saw is never to return. Tomorrow is not guaranteed! Was it a day or perhaps a thousand? I cannot tell. When did it begin and when will it end? Man's days are short and full of trouble, full of wonder, full of joy, and full of pain. But somehow, we find a way to say thank you to our Creator for each new day. So, whether I live to be three score and ten or not, or more, I can truly say, God, my time is in Your Hands."
>
> ~Myra P.

When we look at the longevity of existence for mankind, we learn there has never been a human who has lived a whole day; on God's timeline that is. According to the Bible, even Methuselah, who lived until the age of 969 years old, only lived less than one tenth of a day on God's timeline. Now I must admit 969 years is a long time to live, however, when compared to the Almighty's timeline it's not even close. God is timeless and eternal. His time has no beginning and no ending. Man on this earth is temporary and fleeting. God lives outside of our time.

We have to look at the idea 2 Peter 3:8 brings to mind when speaking about God's timeline versus our timeline: *"...that one day is with the Lord as a thousand years, and a thousand years as one day."* This scripture has been viewed as a representative of the mind of God and not a literal calendar timeline. To further highlight the scripture, God is demonstrating His patience with us and His authority over time's control more than a comparison of numerical periods of clockwork. When someone talks about time, it's not always clear what they mean. God does not mark time like we do. All time belongs to God. We do not own or control it.

> *"A thousand years in your sight are like a day that has just gone by, or like a watch in the night."*
> *~Psalm 90:4*

In Psalm 90:4 we see the comparative text to 2 Peter 3:8. Apostle Peter echoed the words Moses expressed in his Psalm of prayer unto the Lord. One thousand years to God is a brief time, while one day can be a long 24-hour period to us… Jesus is Lord over our time. We must relinquish our plans, thoughts, ideas, and priorities to God's will. If He is Lord of all then He must be Lord over our time. This type of living makes our time fruitful.

It brings us great joy and comfort as Christians to know that God is timeless, eternal, and in sync with our timeline—right now. He is transcendent, but not unreachable. He is right here in this moment with us. And because He's in this moment, He can respond to our needs and prayers.

Because God is eternal, He represents the

flip side of man's limited period of time. Our lives are brief and full of highs and lows, but God has always been our rock and strength throughout the ages.

God is a Spirit *(John 4:24)* and is separated eternally from time. Therefore, the Spirit of God is synonymous with timelessness. Whereas, our flesh is marked with an expiration date.

God does not mark time like we do. God's eternal résumé far exceeds the brevity of humankind.

> *"The length of our days is seventy years—or eighty, if we have the strength; yet their span is but trouble and sorrow, for they quickly pass, and we fly away."*
> ~Psalm 90:10
>
> *"From everlasting to everlasting, You are God."*
> ~Psalm 90:2

He always was and always will be.

So, since God does not mark time as we do, what is the difference between God's time and man's time? We need to know this because when someone talks about time, it's not always clear what they mean.

Time is broken down into two ancient Greek words called Chronos and Kairos. First, let's take a look at Chronos time.

> *"So, teach us to number our days, that we may apply our hearts unto wisdom."*
>
> ~Psalm 90:12

Chronos Time

The alarm sounds. It's 6:00 a.m. on Monday. It's time to rise and shine. Your thoughts span from the hour it takes you to rush out of the door to how much time it will take to prepare for your meetings before lunch. You count down the minutes left until it's time to go home: 3 hours – 45 minutes – 5 minutes, and so on. Every thought from the above scenario is measured in Chronos time. We define our time in a 24-hour day, which is further broken down into smaller increments of measure: minutes, seconds, moments, and so on.

The writer in Psalm 90:12 says,

> "teach us to number our days, that we may apply our hearts unto wisdom."

Being aware of our time and its limitations is an honorable thing. However, we must learn to ask God for a heart of wisdom so we can be taught, like Moses, to understand how brief our days are on this earth. All while being good stewards of the time He gives us and making good earthly decisions that will yield eternal blessings for us personally and for God's Kingdom!

Of all the hardest things to quantify, the numbering of our days is the hardest. We do not know the day the Lord will take us home. We can count seasons, moments, occasions, and even memories, but not the number of our days. "Chronos forms words like "chronological," "chronology," and "chronoscope," which refer to the order of time: clock time, time that is sequential, time that can be measured in intervals, and amounts."[1]

In ancient folklore, there is an expression called "Old Father Time." "Father Time is a human representation of time itself. He symbolizes the abstract concept of time, as well as the constant, one-way movement of time." [2] You may have seen pictures in story books as a child of very old men holding a sickle, used to cut grass, and an hourglass, with sand falling from the top of the glass to the bottom. We know what it means when the last grain of sand falls to the bottom. It means time is up; it's over; you are finished; you are done!

The symbolism of "Old Father Time" does not bring feelings of comfort and joy, despite typically being seen around the winter holidays. Whether or not you grew up hearing childhood folklore or not, the symbol of "Old Father Time" reminds us time is passing by; that is, Chronos time, or time as we know it, is windig down with each passing year.

Let us look to the Word of God for examples of Chronos time.

"And God said, let there be lights in the firmament of the heaven to divide the day from the night; and let them be for signs, and for seasons, and for days, and years: And let them be for lights in the firmament of the heaven to give light upon the earth: and it was so. And God made two great lights; the greater light to rule the day, and the lesser light to rule the night: he made the stars also. And God set them in the firmament of the heaven to give light upon the earth, And to rule over the day and over the night, and to divide the light from the darkness: and God saw that it was good. And the evening and the morning were the fourth day."
Genesis 1:14-19

"See then that ye walk circumspectly, not as fools, but as wise, Redeeming the time, because the days are evil."
~Ephesians 5:15-16

"I am Alpha and Omega, the beginning and the ending, saith the

Lord, which is, and which was, and which is to come, the Almighty."
~Revelation 1:8

God created Chronos time for humans. The Bible says God is "the Alpha and Omega; the beginning and the end" (Revelation 22:13). Chronos time is the glue that ties together Alpha, the beginning, and Omega, the end. Chronos time exists between the beginning and the end. In the above scriptures, we can see the motion, passing, and fluidity of time. Chronos is on the move!

Chronos Time Defined

Time has always been defined according to several aspects, including a period, an age, a lifetime, seasons, or a duration of time. Periods, seasons, or moments refer to the length of time, as in how long something is available. Things such as a sale in your favorite clothing store, the time of the year, or the progression of centuries, decades, years, days, hours, or minutes.

An age, as in "the age of the dinosaurs," refers to a point in history or chronology.

Lifetime, which is very personal to us as humans, refers to the cycle or length of time over the duration of the life God allows us to live. "Duration is the existence or continuation of time."[3]

Time can also be the repetition of occurrences, as in "time and time again," like when your honor roll child gets "A's" continuously.

Kairos Time

However, when God steps into time, or Eternity coincides with time, it becomes Kairos. "Kairos" means "an appointed time, an opportune moment, or a due season."[4] Kairos, unlike Chronos, cannot be measured. It is not quantitative. Rather, "Kairos" is qualitative, or measured by quality, meaning a season, an opportune time, or a right moment in time.

For example, sharing the Gospel of Jesus Christ is a Kairos moment. Taking a breath or a pause is a Kairos moment. An appointed time to reap a blessing is a Kairos moment.

To clarify the difference between the two times, Chronos and Kairos don't run concurrently. The fact that God is not on our timetable can be very frustrating to us, especially when we are playing the "waiting game" and are concerned with schedules, punching time clocks, patterns, hours, and minutes. However, God is not in a hurry!

Let's look to the God's Word for examples of Kairos time.

> *"For the vision is yet for an appointed time, but at the end it shall speak, and not lie: though it tarry, wait for it; because it will surely come, it will not tarry."*
> *~Habakkuk 2:3*

> *"Is anything too hard for the LORD? At the time appointed I will return unto thee, according to the time of life, and Sarah shall have a son. Is anything too hard for the LORD? I will return to you at the appointed time next year, and Sarah will have a son."*
> *~Genesis 18:14*

Parable of the Wheat and the Tares is Kairos Time

"Another parable put he forth unto them, saying, The kingdom of heaven is likened unto a man which sowed good seed in his field: But while men slept, his enemy came and sowed tares among the wheat, and went his way. But when the blade was sprung up, and brought forth fruit, then appeared the tares also. So the servants of the householder came and said unto him, Sir, didst not thou sow good seed in thy field? from whence then hath it tares? He said unto them, An enemy hath done this.

The servants said unto him, Wilt thou then that we go and gather them up? But he said, Nay; lest while ye gather up the tares, ye root up also the wheat with them. Let both grow together until the harvest: and in the time of harvest I will say to the reapers, Gather ye together first the tares, and bind

them in bundles to burn them: but gather the wheat into my barn."
　　　　　~Matthew 13:24-30.

The Return of the Lord in Kairos

"Now we beseech you, brethren, by the coming of our Lord Jesus Christ, and by our gathering together unto him, That ye be not soon shaken in mind, or be troubled, neither by spirit, nor by word, nor by letter as from us, as that the day of Christ is at hand.

Let no man deceive you by any means: for that day shall not come, except there come a falling away first, and that man of sin be revealed, the son of perdition."
　　　　　~2 Thessalonians 2:1-3

The Right Time is a Kairos Moment

"To everything there is a season, and a time to every purpose under the heaven."
　　　　　~Ecclesiastes 3:1

Trusting God in Kairos

"Go to now, ye that say, Today or tomorrow we will go into such a city, and continue there a year, and buy and sell, and get gain: Whereas ye know not what shall be on the morrow. For what is your life? It is even a vapour, that appeareth for a little time, and then vanisheth away. For that ye ought to say, If the Lord will, we shall live, and do this, or that."

~James 4:13-15 ESV

Timing Belongs to God

Time has never been in our control. Remember 2 Peter 3:8?

"But, beloved, be not ignorant of this one thing, that one day is with the Lord as a thousand years, and a thousand years as one day."

Those who live solely by man's time are not under Christ's Lordship. Even though Chronos time was created for our understanding, we must allow Christ to be Lord over our time as we wait for those perfect, divinely appointed moments of Kairos in our lifespan.

"The glory of this present house will be greater than the glory of the former house,' says the LORD Almighty. 'And in this place I will grant peace,' declares the LORD Almighty."

~Haggai 2:9

Chapter 2

The Necessity of Waiting on God's Timing

> *"The promises of God are yea and amen. The promised deposit of a better future and a brighter tomorrow. A surety of hopes not deferred. Oh, how I long for His Glory to illuminate the latter as the former fades into the darkness! The latter shall be greater than the former."*
>
> ~ *Myra P.*

In chapter 1 of the book of Haggai, God gives Zerubbabel and Joshua a message for the Jews, who were the former exiles of Babylon for 70 years. The Lord said it was time to rebuild the Temple. The problem was, the people came against God's timing; they leaned on their own understanding and fashioned all kinds of excuses for disobeying God. The exiles had been back in Jerusalem for 18 years, but the work of rebuilding the Temple lay idle for 14 years prior.

The Lord spoke through Haggai to remind the people that they had been living in beautiful homes with all the comforts, but the House of God lay in ruins.

At the time of Haggai's prophecy, the foundation of the Temple was laid and the altar was rebuilt, but the Temple was not yet rebuilt, so God said it was time to complete the work! Even Solomon made sure he built the Lord's house (1 Kings 6) before he built his own palace (1 Kings 7).

The people could not speak against the Temple being rebuilt, so they spoke against the timing. As a result, God moved against the remnant and their land.

Everything they attempted to do failed, including their crops, causing them to starve, thirst, and have no clothes or wages.

> "Now therefore, thus says the LORD of hosts: "Consider your ways! You have sown much, and bring in little; You eat, but do not have enough; You drink, but you are not filled with drink; You clothe yourselves, but no one is warm; And he who earns wages, Earns wages to put into a bag with holes."
> ~Haggai 1:5-6

> "And I called for a drought upon the land, and upon the mountains, and upon the corn, and upon the new wine, and upon the oil, and upon that which the ground bringeth forth, and upon men, and upon cattle, and upon all the labour of the hands.

> Then Zerubbabel the son of Shealtiel, and Joshua the son of Josedech, the high priest, with all the remnant of the people, obeyed the voice of the LORD their God, and the words of Haggai the prophet, as the LORD

their God had sent him, and the people did fear before the LORD.

Then spake Haggai, the LORD'S messenger in the LORD'S message unto the people, saying, I am with you, saith the LORD.

And the LORD stirred up the spirit of Zerubbabel the son of Shealtiel, governor of Judah, and the spirit of Joshua the son of Josedech, the high priest, and the spirit of all the remnant of the people; and they came and did work in the house of the LORD of hosts, their God,

In the four and twentieth day of the sixth month, in the second year of Darius the king."
~Haggai 1:11-15

God tells the people THINK! What are you doing? My house is laying in waste.

"Thus saith the Lord of hosts; Consider your ways."
~Haggai 1:7

God has appointed times for events to start and stop. His plan for the rebuilding of the Temple was definitely part of His divine calendar.

The truth of the matter was, they simply lost their focus!

God continues to speak through Haggai to Zerubbabel, Joshua, and the remnant. He asked them an important question. The Lord asked, "Who is left among you that saw this house in her first glory? And how do you see it now? Is it not in your eyes in comparison of it as nothing?" (Haggai 2:3). "I will fill this house with glory" (verse 7c). "The glory of the latter house shall be greater than of the former, saith the Lord of hosts" (verse 9).

So, what can we learn from this minor prophetic book? One of the central verses in Haggai is found in Chapter 2 Verse 9a, which says, "the glory of the latter house shall be greater than the former." I believe this is a central message of God's Word. It is also a life-sustaining comfort that helps us journey through the woes of life; knowing that no matter what trials you go through, things will get better. Nothing stays the same. God's promises are "yea and amen." To God be all the Glory!

When we are willing to wait on our Creator, it demonstrates that we are willing to allow God to sit in the driver's seat while we become the passengers. As passengers, we are aware that we give up total control of a moving vehicle. For some of us, that's a hard thing to do, especially in light of the fact that it was God who gave us free will in the first place.

The Bible is filled with many examples of people who waited on God for their latter days to be greater than their former ones.

Examples of People in the Bible Who Waited on God
Job

The story of Job is the perfect example of patience under fire! Job is a very familiar text among both the young and the old. Its theme, "Why Do the Righteous Suffer," is a paradox of complexity in that how can one be righteous, as in right, and be wrong, as in suffer? Job 1, begins in the heavenly realm, where Satan makes a bold statement accusing Job of serving God solely because God has a hedge of protection around him.

> *"Now there was a day when the sons of God came to present themselves before the LORD, and Satan came also among them.*
>
> *And the LORD said unto Satan, Whence comest thou? Then Satan answered the LORD, and said, From going to and fro in the earth, and from walking up and down in it.*
>
> *And the LORD said unto Satan, Hast thou considered my servant Job, that there is none like him in the earth, a perfect and an upright man, one that feareth God, and escheweth evil?*
>
> *Then Satan answered the LORD, and said, Doth Job fear God for nought?*

Hast not thou made an hedge about him, and about his house, and about all that he hath on every side? thou hast blessed the work of his hands, and his substance is increased in the land.

But put forth thine hand now, and touch all that he hath, and he will curse thee to thy face. And the LORD said unto Satan, Behold, all that he hath is in thy power; only upon himself put not forth thine hand. So, Satan went forth from the presence of the LORD."

~Job 1:6-12

This was the beginning of Job's sorrows. From this point on, Job's life, as he knew it, began to fall apart. He lost his animals, his servants, and his children.

"Then Job arose, and rent his mantle, and shaved his head, and fell down upon the ground, and worshipped And said, Naked came I out of my mother's womb, and naked shall I return thither: the LORD gave, and

> *the LORD hath taken away; blessed be the name of the LORD."*
>
> *~Job 1:20-21*

As remarkable as Job's reaction seems, this is not the patience part. Job waited for days for relief, yet he never charged God with unrighteousness. Even when his friends judged him and accused him of being in sin, even when his wife told him to just curse God and die, even when Job was afflicted with the plague of boils, causing him more anguish and torment, he remained faithful. Job continually passed the test by remaining upright.

Being human, Job must have wondered if and when this would all come to an end. We know Job was patient because the book of James says,

> *"Behold, we count them happy which endure. Ye have heard of the patience of Job, and have seen the end of the Lord; that the Lord is very pitiful, and of tender mercy."*
>
> *~James 5:11*

> *"In all this Job sinned not, nor charged God foolishly."*
>
> *~Job 1:22*

Job's patience was rewarded, for God restored everything to him and gave him double for his trouble.

> *"And the LORD turned the captivity of Job, when he prayed for his friends: Also, the LORD gave Job twice as much as he had before.*
>
> *Then came there unto him all his brethren, and all his sisters, and all they that had been of his acquaintance before, and did eat bread with him in his house: and they bemoaned him, and comforted him over all the evil that the LORD had brought upon him: every man also gave him a piece of money, and everyone an earring of gold.*
>
> *So, the LORD blessed the latter end of Job more than his beginning: for he had fourteen thousand sheep, and six thousand camels,*

and a thousand yoke of oxen, and a thousand she asses.

He had also seven sons and three daughters. And he called the name of the first, Jemima; and the name of the second, Kezia; and the name of the third, Kerenhappuch.

And in all the land were no women found so fair as the daughters of Job: and their father gave them inheritance among their brethren.

After this lived Job a hundred and forty years, and saw his sons, and his sons' sons, even four generations.

So, Job died, being old and full of days."
~Job 42:10-17

So, Job's latter days became greater than his former days.

The life of David is another familiar text among young and old where we see the importance of waiting on God's timing.

David

The Appointing

1 Samuel 16 tells the story of young David, who was chosen by God to be Saul's successor after Saul disobeyed God's strict commands to kill all the Amalekites (I Samuel 15:9).

Even though David was a mere lad at the time he was anointed, many years passed before he began to rule as king. It may seem obvious why God made David wait to rule, being that he was a minor; however, let's look deeper into the text. There is always a reason for the gap between the promise and the blessing.

> *"And he said, Peaceably: I am come to sacrifice unto the LORD: sanctify yourselves, and come with me to the sacrifice. And he sanctified Jesse and his sons, and called them to the sacrifice. And it came to pass, when they were come, that he looked on Eliab, and said, Surely the LORD'S anointed is before him. But the LORD said unto Samuel, Look*

not on his countenance, or on the height of his stature; because I have refused him: for the LORD seeth not as man seeth; for man looketh on the outward appearance, but the LORD looketh on the heart.

Then Jesse called Abinadab, and made him pass before Samuel. And he said, Neither hath the LORD chosen this.

Then Jesse made Shammah to pass by. And he said, Neither hath the LORD chosen this. Again, Jesse made seven of his sons to pass before Samuel. And Samuel said unto Jesse, The LORD hath not chosen these.

And Samuel said unto Jesse, Are here all thy children? And he said, There remaineth yet the youngest, and, behold, he keepeth the sheep. And Samuel said unto Jesse, Send and fetch him: for we will not sit down till he come hither. "And he sent, and brought him in. Now he was ruddy, and withal of a beautiful

> *countenance, and goodly to look to. And the LORD said, Arise, anoint him: for this is he.* "*Then Samuel took the horn of oil, and anointed him in the midst of his brethren: and the Spirit of the Lord came upon David from that day forward.*"
> ~I Samuel 16:5-13

Young David was chosen, anointed, and eventually appointed above his brothers. He didn't look like a king, but God saw his heart. It took nearly 15 years from the time he was anointed king to the time he actually became king! How long have you been in the "waiting game"? Perhaps God wants you to be prepared for the process in the same way as David.

God wanted to prepare David for leadership through the process of refining. In other words, God needed to tear some things down and build some things up, in and through David. While God will bless us by speaking into our lives, we still have to be made ready. There is nothing redeeming about prematurity. A tree that tries to bear fruit before its time is going to either bear bad fruit or none at all. God wanted to prepare David to be humble, love the people, and obey God. He was being primed and as such, he went through many trials including defeating Goliath, being banished by Saul, having to hide in the desert, living on the run, being forced to face his own sins, and fighting many battles.

Defeating Goliath

After he was anointed as Israel's next king, David fought and defeated Goliath.

> *"Thy servant slew both the lion and the bear: and this uncircumcised Philistine shall be as one of them, seeing he hath defied the armies of the living God. David said moreover, The LORD that delivered me out of the paw of the lion, and out of the paw of the bear, he will deliver me out of the hand of this Philistine. And Saul said unto David, Go, and the LORD be with thee."*
> *~I Samuel 17:36-37*

"So, David prevailed with over the

> *Philistine with a sling and a stone, and struck the Philistine and killed him. But there was no sword in the hand of David."*
>
> *v. 50*

Little did young David know that by tending to the sheep, it was a waiting period of preparation.

In shepherding the flock, God was preparing David to fight, win, and shepherd the people.

> *"And David said unto Saul...Thy servant kept his father's sheep, and there came a lion, and a bear, and took a lamb of the flock: And I went out after him, and smote him, and delivered it out of his mouth: and when he arose against me, I caught him by his beard, and smote him, and slew him. Thy servant slew both the lion and the bear: and this uncircumcised Philistine shall be as one of them, seeing he hath defied the armies of the living God."*
>
> *~I Samuel 17:34-36*

Being Tormented by Saul

After David and the soldiers returned from killing the Philistine, the women sang and danced throughout Israel, crediting David with slaying more than Saul.

Saul, being a paranoid person, began to watch David's every move from that point forward. Anger and jealousy, fueled by an evil spirit, took control of Saul. He tried and failed several times to kill David.

Saul threw a spear at David three times and missed him each time (I Samuel 18:11; 19:10). Saul then told his son Jonathan and his officers to kill David. Saul offers his daughter, Merab, to David in marriage in exchange for his fighting in the "Lord's Battles," hoping he would get killed (I Samuel 18:17).

Merab was given to another in marriage, but Micah, Saul's other daughter, loved David. Saul agreed to this marriage, believing that she would be a snare to David, causing the Philistines to kill him. In order to marry the king's daughter, which pleased

David, King Saul told him he must bring the foreskins of 200 Philistines.

> *"Again, Saul was hoping that David would get killed but he prevailed. Saul grew more and more afraid of David because he saw clearly that the Lord was with him. The more David fought, the more he prevailed because God was with him!"*
> ~I Samuel 18:28-30

In 1 Samuel 20:1c, David asked Jonathan a natural question, "What have I done? What is mine iniquity? And what is my sin before thy father, that he seeks my life?

David was on the run, having to hide in the deserts of Moan (I Samuel 23), Engedi (I Samuel 24), and Ziph (I Samuel 26), all while waiting for his promise to serve as king to be fulfilled.

David's Sins

II Samuel 11 tells the account of David and Bathsheba. David decided to send Joab, his servants, and all of Israel into battle, while he remained home, with the goal of destroying the Ammonites. It's hard not to look at the timing of the flow of these events.

> *"And it came to pass in an eveningtide, that David arose from off his bed, and walked upon the roof of the king's house: and from the roof he saw a woman washing herself; and the woman was very beautiful to look upon.*
>
> *And David sent and enquired after the woman. And one said, Is not this Bathsheba, the daughter of Eliam, the wife of Uriah the Hittite?*
>
> *And David sent messengers, and took her; and she came in unto him, and he lay with her; for she was purified from her uncleanness: and she returned unto her house. And the woman conceived, and sent and told David, and said, I am with child."*
> ~II Samuel 11:2-5

Now, David knew he had sinned and tried to devise a scheme to cover his sin. David clearly did not count the cost. He didn't stop to see the end from the beginning. He allowed his flesh to rule in the absence of righteousness.

David asked Joab to send Uriah the Hittite to him, verses 7-8c...

> *"And when Uriah was come unto him, David demanded of him how Joab did, and how the people did, and how the war prospered. And David said to Uriah, Go down to thy house, and wash thy feet."*

David was a master at strategizing and had proven he was able to get out of dangerous and sticky situations, but not this time!

> *"And Uriah departed out of the king's house, and there followed him a mess of meat from the king. But Uriah slept at the door of the king's house with all the servants of his lord, and went not down to his house. And when they had told David, saying, Uriah went not down unto his house"*
>
> vv. 8d-9

Uriah made a decision to not go home and lay down with his wife, but instead chose to honor his commitment to battle. Because Uriah did not sleep with his wife, she could not be carrying her husband's child, and the truth would surely come out.

> *"David said unto Uriah, Camest thou not from thy journey? why then didst thou not go down unto thine house?*
>
> *And Uriah said unto David, The ark, and Israel, and Judah, abide in tents; and my lord Joab, and the servants of my lord, are encamped in the open fields; shall I then go into mine house, to eat and to drink, and to lie with my wife? as thou livest, and as thy soul liveth, I will not do this thing. And David said to Uriah, Tarry here today also, and tomorrow I will let thee depart.*
>
> *So, Uriah abode in Jerusalem that day, and the morrow. And when David had called him, he did eat and drink before him; and he made*

> *him drunk: and at even he went out to lie on his bed with the servants of his lord, but went not down to his house."*
>
> *vv. 10d-13 KJV*

This was David's second failed attempt to cover his sin with Bathsheba. Uriah still did not go home to lay with his wife.

> *"And it came to pass in the morning, that David wrote a letter to Joab, and sent it by the hand of Uriah. And he wrote in the letter, saying, Set ye Uriah in the forefront of the hottest battle, and retire ye from him, that he may be smitten, and die. And it came to pass, when Joab observed the city, that he assigned Uriah unto a place where he knew that valiant men were. And the men of the city went out, and fought with Joab: and there fell some of the people of the servants of David; and Uriah the Hittite died also."*
>
> *vv.14-17*

Oh, what a tangled mess of tragedy! This

was only the beginning of a downward cascade of woes for David and his family. As a result of David's knavery, he subjected his family, the nation, and himself to a season of retribution from God Almighty.

David's uncontrolled adultery produced an unwanted pregnancy, laced with multiple attempts to cover it up, ending with the murder of an innocent man of integrity. The tragedies don't end here. His baby did not live. His daughter, Tamar, was raped by her brother. Sibling rivalry ended with one brother killing the other and one of his sons' behaviors causing the apostasy of much of Israel.

These were difficult days for David, but they were also times of maturation.

David became one of the best kings ever because of the trials and tribulations he endured. David's seasons of on-going boot camp trained him to deal with perilous situations, and how to fight and conquer. He learned to depend upon God, to love His Holy Word, and to love God with his whole heart.

He learned obedience and submission, even when his life was in danger.

He developed close, enduring friendships and alliances and learned to honor the anointing of God. Even in David's bouts of fear and terror at the hands of Saul, Absalom, and Achish, David grew to fear and revere the Lord.

And, out of all these twists and turns, David left us with the masterful genre of the book of Psalms. These Psalms stir the deepest gamut of emotional highs and lows. They direct our gaze upward in adoration and praise to our Most Holy and Righteous God.

This is generally God's pattern for preparation. He calls us to be faithful right where we are and then uses our faithfulness to accomplish greater things. If David had run scared of the lion or the bear, he would never have been ready to fight Goliath. But he was faithful then, so he will be faithful now.

"His lord said unto him, Well done,

> *good and faithful servant; thou hast been faithful over a few things, I will make thee ruler over many things: enter thou into the joy of thy lord."*
>
> ~*Matthew 25:23*

All the time David spent protecting the sheep from bears and lions was actually a time of waiting and preparation. As he waited for his appointed time to rule, it was not wasted time. God was preparing this shepherd boy to become a king who would qualify to shepherd the nation of Israel.

> *"For who hath despised the day of small things?"*
>
> ~*Zechariah 4:10*

As we look at how David's life has produced eternal lessons and blessings for all of God's people, his latter was greater than his former.

He started out as a shepherd boy and became a forerunner of the Good Shepherd, Jesus Christ. God had promised David that there would always be a descendant from the house of David to sit on the throne.

> *"And thine house and thy kingdom shall be established for ever before thee: thy throne shall be established forever."*
> *~II Samuel 7:16*

David says in Psalm 40:1-3,

> *"I waited patiently for the LORD; and he inclined unto me, and heard my cry. He brought me up also out of an horrible pit, out of the miry clay, and set my feet upon a rock, and established my goings".*
>
> *And he hath put a new song in my mouth, even praise unto our God: many shall see it, and fear, and shall trust in the LORD."*

Whatever you are waiting on God to do, your latter shall be greater than the former.

In the book of Haggai, the people needed patience to wait on God to refocus them so they could build God's house. Job, waited with patience for God to restore him. In I Samuel, David waited on God's appointed time to lead the Kingdom of Israel. The list of those who waited on God's timing is endless.

In Genesis 29:28, Jacob waited 14 years to marry Rachel after being tricked by Laban.

> "And Jacob did so, and fulfilled her week: and he gave him Rachel his daughter to wife also."

Simeon waited on the baby Jesus to be born in the Gospel of Luke 2:26. Jesus waited about 30 years to begin His earthly ministry. Baptized by John the Baptist at age 30, His ministry lasted about three years. Jesus was obedient to Levitical law, which states,

> "From thirty years old and upward until fifty years old shalt thou number them; all that enter in to perform the service, to do the work in the tabernacle of the congregation."
> ~Numbers 4:23

This was in order to keep in line with the

priestly requirements of the old covenant, which is fulfilled in Jesus.

The Apostles waited for the promise of the baptism of the Holy Spirit (Acts 1:4–5). The saints are waiting on the redemption of our bodies (Romans 8:23).

Whatever you are waiting for God to do, the latter will be greater than the former!

Why it's So Hard to Wait on God?

It's hard to wait on God because our flesh wants what it wants. Wow! Where have I heard that before? Our flesh is the source of the blame. It is untamed, selfish, and hard to control.

> *"For the desires of the flesh are against the Spirit."*
> *~Galatians 5:17*

If you want to build a powerful home front, you must begin with building your Spirit, or your inner man.

> *"Like a city whose walls are broken*

through is a person who lacks self-control."

~Proverbs 25:28

"He that is slow to anger is better than the mighty; and he that ruleth his spirit than he that taketh a city. The lot is cast into the lap; but the whole disposing thereof is of the LORD."

~Proverbs 16:32-33

"For the mind that is set on the flesh is hostile to God, for it does not submit to God's law; indeed, it cannot."

~Romans 8:7

"Be patient, then, brothers and sisters, until the Lord's coming. See how the farmer waits for the land to yield its valuable crop, patiently waiting for the autumn and spring rains. You too, be patient and stand firm, because the Lord's coming is near."

~James 5:7

It's a testament against the Christian character, but waiting on God is not something that most of us relish. It almost feels as though we are being punished and committed to serve a life sentence for the most heinous crime. The more anxious we are, the less we want to wait. With every twist and turn, we just want out of the "waiting game."

Agitation and frustration rushes in like a flood every time we have to wait on line at a bank or on a movie theatre line.

Don't get stuck in traffic! Besides making you late, it can ruin your whole mood having to listen to the sounds of blaring horns, unspeakable language, and inhaling the sickening fumes that seem to make you feel as though you have been poisoned.

Even going to the doctor's office can almost make you feel sicker than what is actually ailing you.

> *"And therefore, will the LORD wait, that he may be gracious unto you, and therefore will he be exalted,*

> *that he may have mercy upon you: for the LORD is a God of judgment: blessed are all they that wait for him."*
>
> ~Isaiah 30:18

So Why is Waiting on God So Necessary?

As difficult as it is to wait on God, it is necessary! Knowing why it's needed might help us bear the burdens of waiting. Waiting places parameters on our thoughts so we can stay focused during the pauses of life. We can see from God's Word that waiting on God helps in many ways.

Waiting Makes Us Strong

> *"Wait on the LORD: be of good courage, and he shall strengthen thine heart: wait, I say, on the LORD."*
>
> ~Psalm 27:14

Waiting Helps Us Look To The Lord

> *"Behold, as the eyes of servants look*

unto the hand of their masters, and as the eyes of a maiden unto the hand of her mistress; so our eyes wait upon the LORD our God, until that he have mercy upon us."
~Psalm 123:2

Waiting Blesses Us

"And therefore will the LORD wait, that he may be gracious unto you, and therefore will he be exalted, that he may have mercy upon you: for the LORD is a God of judgment: blessed are all they that wait for him".
~Isaiah 30:18

Nature Is Our Example

"Be patient therefore, brethren, unto the coming of the Lord. Behold, the husbandman waiteth for the precious fruit of the earth, and hath long patience for it, until he receive the early and latter rain. Be ye also patient; stablish your hearts: for the coming of the Lord draweth nigh."
~James 5:7-8

Waiting Helps Us Stay Ready

"Let your loins be girded about, and your lights burning; And ye yourselves like unto men that wait for their lord, when he will return from the wedding; that when he cometh and knocketh, they may open unto him immediately.

Blessed are those servants, whom the lord when he cometh shall find watching: verily I say unto you, that he shall gird himself, and make them to sit down to meat, and will come forth and serve them.

And if he shall come in the second watch, or come in the third watch, and find them so, blessed are those servants.

And this know, that if the goodman of the house had known what hour the thief would come, he would have watched, and not have suffered his house to be broken through. Be ye therefore ready also: for the Son of

> *man cometh at an hour when ye think not."*
>
> *~Luke 12:35-40*

Waiting Helps Us Surrender to God

This is because when we wait, the Lord will fight for us!

> *"And Moses said unto the people, Fear ye not, stand still, and see the salvation of the LORD, which he will shew to you today: for the Egyptians whom ye have seen today, ye shall see them again no more forever. The LORD shall fight for you, and ye shall hold your peace."*
>
> *~Exodus 14:14*

> *"Looking for that blessed hope, and the glorious appearing of the great God and our Savior Jesus Christ."*
>
> *~Titus 2:13*

"So, teach us to number our days, That we may apply our hearts unto wisdom."

~Psalm 90:12

Chapter 3

Perspectives of Time

> *"As I run off the bus towards the schoolyard fence, I realize I'm later than I think and class is beginning to commence. Then I remember, "I'm not in control!" It was the bus driver's fault after all!"*
>
> ~Myra P

Have you ever taken the time to think about time? No, it's not a trick question! Time and waiting are so intertwined, they can never be separated by man. Only God can separate them.

The Bible tells us about an act of God when

the sun stood still and the moon stopped.

> "Then spake Joshua to the LORD in the day when the LORD delivered up the Amorites before the children of Israel, and he said in the sight of Israel, Sun, stand thou still upon Gibeon; And thou, Moon, in the valley of rAjalon. And the sun stood still, and the moon stayed, Until the people had avenged themselves upon their enemies. Is not this written in the book of Jashur? So the sun stood still in the midst of heaven, And hasted not to go down about a whole day. And there was no day like that before it or after it, that the LORD hearkened unto the voice of a man: for the LORD fought for Israel."
> ~Joshua 10:12-14

The Waiting Room

When one thinks of time, they think of "the wait." How long do I have to wait? How long will I be sick? When can I retire? and so on. Even at this present time, we are waiting for COVID and wearing masks to come to an end. Emotions start to flare from being overwhelmed by the thought of things staying the same. We are challenged on every side—spiritually, socially, physically, and mentally—when we defer to our carnal philosophies for an answer that only God can provide. See, since God is the Author and Finisher of all creation, then shouldn't a wise man ask the Creator about His creations? When we begin to understand how God views time, we can begin to take caution in how we conduct our lives.

Let's look at Psalm 90 to learn how our God views time, and maybe then we can get an understanding of the waiting dilemma.

So, how does God view time? There are many things that are common to man, but time is not well understood. It's said that practice makes perfect, but practicing time or waiting for time to pass is not one of them. We must look to God, who is the Creator of time, for some sort of understanding.

When I read Psalm 90, the phrase "glass half full; glass half empty" comes to mind. In other words, your perspective determines your conclusion about the glass's volume of liquid. If you see it half full, then you are an optimist, and if you see it half empty, then you are a pessimist.

Well, just like these two perspectives have different conclusions, so do God and man when it comes to timing. God sees time differently than we do. His perspective is different; therefore, His conclusion is also.

> *"For my thoughts are not your thoughts, neither are your ways my ways, saith the LORD."*
> ~Isaiah 55:8-9

In Chapter 1 of this book, "The Difference Between God's Timing and Man's Timing," I spoke about the differences between God's time (Kairos) and man's time (Chronos). Kairos time is a set period of time, a breath, or a moment of silence. It is time that is not measured in quantity, phases, or numbers. Chronos time is chronological time. It is time that can be measured by clocks, watches, months, days, and years; it is time that moves forward.

Perspectives of Time

Psalm 90 is a prayer that Moses prayed to God, expressing the awesomeness of the Almighty's ownership of time!

- Moses acknowledges God as his home. He declares God's eternity and stability down through many long generations (v.1).

- God is the Alpha and Omega. He has no beginning and no end (v. 2).

- God has the control and power to give life and then take it away (vs 3). God is on an eternal timetable, but our lives pass quickly (v. 4).

- Our lives are fleeting like the blades of grass (v. 5-6).

- God has numbered our time. Man has a short life and may live 70 years, and 80 if God allows (v. 9-10).

- Because man's days are short, Moses asks God to teach us to number our days so we cna grow in wisdom. (v. 12)

The final six verses of Psalm 90 remind

us to count and use our time wisely. It's not enough to know that our time here is brief but, what are we doing with the earthly timeline we call a life span? Especially since Moses has so eloquently contrasted God's and our perspectives on time.

What does this Psalm teach us about how God views time and how we should conduct our lives?

Take a moment to pause and read the rest of Psalm 90...

> *"So teach us to number our days, that we may apply our hearts unto wisdom. Return, O LORD, how long? and let it repent thee concerning thy servants.*
>
> *O satisfy us early with thy mercy; that we may rejoice and be glad all our days.*
>
> *Make us glad according to the days wherein thou hast afflicted us, and the years wherein we have seen evil.*

Let thy work appear unto thy servants, and thy glory unto their children.

And let the beauty of the LORD our God be upon us: and establish thou the work of our hands upon us; yea, the work of our hands establish thou it."

vv. 12-17

See, our disappointments come from our desires not being met.

By the way, maybe the bus driver wasn't at fault at all. Maybe I needed to catch an earlier bus. Maybe I needed to get up earlier. Maybe I should have gone to bed sooner!

"And therefore, will the Lord wait that he may be gracious unto you, and therefore will he be exalted that he may have mercy upon you: for the Lord is a God of Judgment. Blessed are all they that wait for him."

~Isaiah 30:18

Chapter 4

Waiting Grace

> "Gracious grace is your name. So wonderful is your name! I tarry at your throne of grace, completely unashamed. Waiting for you to come to me, longing for your grace. I come to you as an offering, beholding you face to face. As I mirror your total attributes with full embrace, because you have showered me with your pure grace!"
>
> ~Myra P.

Waiting on God's Timing is a Special Kind of Grace

Gracious is one of my favorite attributes to describe the character of God Almighty.

He is full of grace. Grace is not only who God is, but it's what He does. Every move of God is an example of His grace toward us. From God waking us up in the morning, to our laying down safely at night, and every minute in between, God is gracious.

- God's grace empowers us with the ability to wait on Him and to receive deliverance from all evil.

- God's grace empowers us to wait on Him when we are weak.

- God's grace gives us the ability to endure when the going gets tough.

- God's grace encourages us to wait for His direction when we feel overwhelmed.

- God's grace signifies that He is ruling from His heavenly throne, and that is why we can WAIT!

I love the way Isaiah 30:18 reminds us, God longs to be gracious unto us. He can't wait to shower us with His grace. Wow! He waits for just the right time to do this. He brought deliverance to those in Judah who waited and trusted in Him and not Egypt. As a result, they received His grace.

God wants us to do the same. He is not too early or too late. We are blessed if we wait on Him. It's a nice package of reciprocity. God waits to be gracious toward us, and we wait for Him to be gracious toward us.

Why is this important? Because waiting is necessary, and God will give us the grace to wait. God has to give us the grace to wait because waiting goes against our nature.

Our innate response to waiting is NOT to wait. We don't want any part of it. That is why grace has to be given to us by God. It is a gift of the Spirit that we must receive, just like salvation.

Without grace, we can't do right. Grace is an unmerited favor we don't deserve, so positioning ourselves to wait on top of receiving this gift of grace truly humbles us into a posture of "waiting grace."

There are several reasons why "waiting

grace" is important. Let us examine those reasons through the lens of God's Word.

Waiting Grace is an Act of Pure Obedience

When we have the grace to wait on God, it is our way to show honor and respect toward God.

> *"Having made known unto us the mystery of his will, according to his good pleasure which he hath purposed in himself."*
> *~Ephesians 1:9*

God is Working Behind the Scenes

God sees the end from the beginning. His thoughts and ways are higher than ours.

He guarantees our results like He guaranteed the farmer's harvest of crops in due time. He works according to His timing, not ours.

> *"Be patient, then, brothers and sisters, until the Lord's coming. See how the*

farmer waits for the land to yield its valuable crop, patiently waiting for the autumn and spring rains. You too, be patient and stand firm, because the Lord's coming is near."

~James 5:7

Waiting Grace is Endowed with Divine Power

Having a divine power in and of itself, waiting grace helps us fall in line with God's will.

"Each of you should use whatever gift you have received to serve others, as faithful stewards of God's grace in its various forms."

~1 Peter 4:10

The Grace to Wait is All We Need to Live Through Life's Trials

"But he said to me, "My grace is sufficient for you, for my power is made perfect in weakness. Therefore I will boast all the more gladly about my weaknesses, so

that Christ's power may rest on me."
~2 Corinthians 12:9

Waiting Grace Give Us Power

"And, behold, I send the promise of my Father upon you: but tarry ye in the city of Jerusalem, until ye be endued with power from on high."
~Luke 24:49

Waiting Grace Encourages Patience

Waiting grace is essential whether we are patient with others or with ourselves when we mess up. It helps us to forgive.

"In him we have redemption through his blood, the forgiveness of sins, in accordance with the riches of God's grace that he lavished on us."
~Ephesians 1:7-8

In summary, the grace to wait on God is necessary. It helps us be obedient, patient, have divine power, go through trials, and forgive. There are many other reasons why we must experience waiting grace, but these are just a few. God's grace is exhaustive and extensive.

Let's look at the man at the pool of Bethesda. In John 5:1–15, we read about Jesus and the invalid, who was stuck at the poolside of Bethesda for 38 years.

This man had no hope of getting into the pool to be healed, and he was greatly discouraged. Jesus, however, cured the man just by telling him to get up and walk. This was the result of waiting grace. How inspiring!

It doesn't matter how long you've been waiting for your blessing; if you heed the words of God when you hear Him speak, just as swiftly as the former invalid did, your promise is sure to be fulfilled.

> *"After this there was a feast of the Jews; and Jesus went up to Jerusalem.*
>
> *Now there is at Jerusalem by the sheep market a pool, which is called in the Hebrew tongue Bethesda,*

having five porches.

In these lay a great multitude of impotent folk, of blind, halt, withered, waiting for the moving of the water.

For an angel went down at a certain season into the pool, and troubled the water: whosoever then first after the troubling of the water stepped in was made whole of whatsoever disease he had.

And a certain man was there, which had an infirmity thirty and eight years.

When Jesus saw him lie, and knew that he had been now a long time in that case, he saith unto him, Wilt thou be made whole?

The impotent man answered him, Sir, I have no man, when the water is troubled, to put me into the pool: but while I am coming, another steppeth down before me.

Jesus saith unto him, Rise, take up thy bed, and walk.

And immediately the man was made whole, and took up his bed, and walked: and on the same day was the sabbath.

The Jews therefore said unto him that was cured, It is the sabbath day: it is not lawful for thee to carry thy bed.

He answered them, He that made me whole, the same said unto me, Take up thy bed, and walk. Then asked they him, What man is that which said unto thee, Take up thy bed, and walk?

And he that was healed wist not who it was: for Jesus had conveyed himself away, a multitude being in that place. Afterward Jesus findeth him in the temple, and said unto him, Behold, thou art made whole: sin no more, lest a worse thing come unto thee. The man departed,

> *and told the Jews that it was Jesus, which had made him whole."*
>
> *~John 5:1-15*

The Grace to Wait for Answered Prayer

Daniel's Prayer

In Daniel 10, we see Daniel praying fervently for the Lord to spare Jerusalem's wrath. And although he waited to receive a response 21 days later, we learn in verse 12 that the Lord heard his prayer the same day he petitioned God. He believed God had heard his prayer and that it had already been answered, even though it had not manifested yet.

> *"Then said he unto me, Fear not, Daniel: for from the first day that thou didst set thine heart to understand, and to chasten thyself before thy God, thy words were heard, and I am come for thy words."*
>
> *~Daniel 10:12*

If we allow God to have His will in our lives, we will not only develop the grace to wait, but we will also grow in grace.

God Gives Us Grace to Wait

> *But grow in the grace and knowledge of our Lord and Savior Jesus Christ. To Him be the glory, both now and to the day of eternity. Amen.*
>
> ~2 Peter 3:18

"And therefore will the LORD wait, that he may be gracious unto you, and therefore will he be exalted, that he may have mercy."

~Isaiah 30:18

Chapter 5

God Is Waiting On Us...
God Is Waits Too

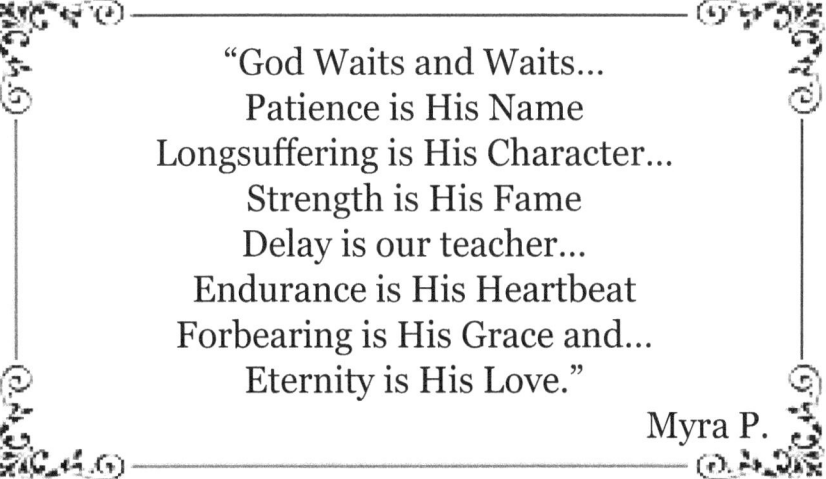

"God Waits and Waits...
Patience is His Name
Longsuffering is His Character...
Strength is His Fame
Delay is our teacher...
Endurance is His Heartbeat
Forbearing is His Grace and...
Eternity is His Love."

Myra P.

When I think back to when I first gave my life to Jesus Christ, at 33 years old, I wondered why I waited so long to make this wonderful decision. I wondered why God didn't seem to be in a hurry to save me or why He just didn't reach down and snatch me up! This was because God was waiting on me!

God understands the emotions waiting drums up for us because He waits too. He waits for us to realize we are sinners, that we are undone, that we need a Savior, and that we are hopeless without Him. So, He waits and waits. I am grateful God waited for me to wake up and know what time it was. Like we say in church, *"He didn't have to do it, but He did!"*

See, God is not going to do everything for us. That is why He waits too. He waits for us to have our, *"come to Jesus moment."* He waits until after we have gone through the trials, mistakes, pain, and pride of self-reliance. When we are sick and tired of being sick and tired and we fall on our knees; ready to surrender all in repentance, that is when God knows His wait for us is over. For some of us, the wait takes longer than for others. But God is patient.

"The Lord is not slack concerning

> *his promise, as some men count slackness; but is longsuffering to us-ward, not willing that any should perish, but that all should come to repentance."*
>
> ~*2 Peter 3:9*

God doesn't wait the same way we do. Our waiting is full of anger, impatience, and doubt. For us, waiting often brings these emotions and attitudes because we are operating in the flesh and totally without faith. Waiting causes disappointment because our desires are not being met.

> *"Hope deferred maketh the heart sick: but when the desire cometh, it is a tree of life."*
>
> ~*Proverbs 13:12*

Also, we tend to compare ourselves to others, which never produces good fruit.

> *"For we dare not make ourselves of the number, or compare ourselves with some that commend themselves: but they measuring themselves by themselves, and*

> *comparing themselves among themselves, are not wise."*
> ~2 Corinthians 10:12

Comparing ourselves to others only leads to a lack of self-worth, degradation, and condemnation. These are not the thoughts God has toward us.

The more we get to know God, our attitude toward waiting should change for the better. When we learn that God has a perfect plan for our lives, when we realize that He makes no mistakes, when we learn that His appointed time or His Kairos moments are divinely orchestrated, then and only then will our attitudes get better. Because we are humans, we will always have the tendency to lose at the "waiting game." However, it will be a lot easier if we remember that while we are waiting on God, He is waiting too!

So then, how does God wait? He waits with patience, endurance, and long-suffering. Why would a Divine and Perfect God want to wait on an imperfect man? Simply put, He loves us and wants to be our example of patience. From the time the first Adam fell causing sin to enter into the world, God has been waiting for man to realize that he is a sinner and that there is a way of escape in the person of Jesus Christ! We must accept Jesus Christ as our Lord and Savior. Even though it has been over 2,000 years since Christ died on the cross for our sins, God is STILL waiting on man to accept His free gift of salvation. How many of us throw in the towel after a brief moment? Perhaps a year or two? Well, not God because He is long suffering toward us, not willing that any should perish but that all souls would heed the call to eternal life with Him.

His waiting is an act of His tender mercies toward us. I know you are wondering how waiting can be an act of God's love for us. When my mother made me wait for something that I really, desperately wanted, I felt a lot of emotions, but love was not one of them! So, I had to think about this issue too. One thing I was sure of was that my mother loved me to pieces. Her love was like no other I had ever experienced in my whole life. I knew she loved me because I knew who she was and who she was to me. Even when I felt she was being too strict with her rules and lists of dos and don'ts, love was always my steady foothold that grounded me and helped me rebound from my attitudes of resistance.

God is no different. We must get to know God; His attributes, His kindness, His everlasting love toward us, and that there is no greater love than the love of our Creator. Yes, even more love than the love of a great mother. Wow!

As I got to know God's character more and more through prayer, fasting, worship, and spending time in His Word, I realized that God is Sovereign. He is El Shaddai, God Almighty, in whom we have all that we need because He is all sufficient, a Comforter, and full of enumerable blessings.

> *"When Abram was 99 years old, ADONAI appeared to Abram, and He said to him, "I am El Shaddai. Continually walk before me and you will be blameless."*
>
> *~Genesis 17:1*

> *"Even by the God of thy father, who*

shall help thee; and by the Almighty, who shall bless thee with blessings of heaven above, blessings of the deep that lieth under, blessings of the breasts, and of the womb."
~Genesis 49:25

God is our Jehovah Shalom, our Peace.

"Then Gideon built an altar there unto the LORD, and called it Jehovah Shalom."
~Judges 6:24

"Peace I leave with you, my peace I give unto you: not as the world giveth, give I unto you. Let not your heart be troubled, neither let it be afraid."
~John 14:27

The Waiting Dilemmas

God has three solutions to our waiting dilemmas: which are NOW, DELAYED, or NEVER. Ah, Now! We love the word NOW! Even a child understands now. Now means we don't have to wait. It means immediate gratification. It means go! We love this response. When we hear NOW, we give God high praises and hallelujahs! We do our dance and clap our hands. All is right in the world.

Then sometimes God will say, DELAYED. "Um wait? What?... Can you repeat that Lord? I don't think I heard you correctly! On my!" We don't quite know what to do with DELAYED. "Delayed until when? How much delay are we talking about? Can you give me a sign Lord?" Oh boy! Here comes the attitude!

But delay is nothing compared to NEVER. Wow! Here is where we totally lose our pure minds!!! Now we somehow find ourselves at the "bargaining table," where we petition God to change His mind; where we offer God a fleece or beg for mercy! We forget that God is omniscient and can see farther and clearer than we can. So, no matter how much we are debased by the word NEVER, we must accept it as an act of love, concern, and Divine protection. We will never know how many angels God has encamped around us as a hedge of protection. Hallelujah!

We find many instances in the Bible of God waiting.

Let's visit some more of those occasions.

- God waited 4 days to raise Lazarus from the dead so the people would believe in how great God is (John 11:43-44).

- God waited to heal until after He dismissed the crowd (Matthew 9:23-26).

- He waited to give Abraham and Sarah a child in order to test their faith (Genesis 21:2 & Hebrews 11:11).

- God waited 14 years to give Jacob the wife of his dreams, Rachel. (Genesis 29:28 KJV). God demonstrated He will bless us if we wait on Him.

- Jacob tricked Esau out of his birthright. (Genesis 25:29-34). Laban tricked the trickster, Jacob (Genesis 29:25-27).

"The Lord is not slack concerning

> *his promise, as some men count slackness; but is longsuffering to us-ward, not willing that any should perish, but that all should come to repentance."*
>
> ~2 Peter 3:9-10

> *"But You, O Lord, are a God merciful and gracious, Slow to anger and abundant in lovingkindness and truth."*
>
> ~Psalm 86:4

You want to see patience? Look at God Almighty! Our God is the ultimate example of patience. When God created the heavens and the earth, he did not immediately create Adam and place him in the Garden of Eden.

Genesis Chapter 1 recounts the sequence of events unveiling the plan of God's provisions.

Day 1 - God created light and separated the light from the darkness, calling light "day" and darkness "night."

Day 2 - God created an expanse to separate the waters and called it "sky."

Day 3 - God created the dry ground and gathered the waters, calling the dry ground "land," and the gathered waters "seas." On day three, God also created vegetation (plants and trees).

Day 4 - God created the sun, moon, and the stars to give light to the earth and to govern and separate the day and the night. These would also serve as signs to mark seasons, days, and years.

Day 5 - God created every living creature of the seas and every winged bird, blessing them to multiply and fill the waters and the sky with life.

Day 6 - God created the animals to fill the earth. God also created man and woman (Adam and Eve) in his own image to commune with Him.

He blessed them and gave them every creature and the whole earth to rule over, care for, and cultivate.

Day 7 - God had finished His work of creation and so He rested on theseventh day, blessing it and making it holy. (Genesis 1:1-2:3)

The wait was finally over! God created a place specifically for His creation.

"I had fainted, unless I had believed to see the goodness of the LORD in the land of the living. Wait on the LORD: be of good courage, and he shall strengthen thine heart: wait, I say, on the LORD."

~Psalm 27:13-14

Chapter 6
Waiting For The Blessing After The Promise

> "A promise is not a promise without the Spirit of the Lord. Believing that waiting will reap a reward.
>
> Clothe yourself with the garments of praise. Position your inner man with courage that stays.
>
> Blessings flow from the promises made, So, posture yourself to receive all He gave!"
> ~Myra P.

I will never forget the title of a sermon I

heard years ago called, "What Do You Do Between the Promise and the Blessing?" Of all the sermons I've heard over the years, and I've heard some good ones, this one has stuck with me until now. It has become a part of me because it made me think. I mean, isn't that what a sermon is supposed to do? Besides the fact that this sermon's title caught my attention and made me think, it has caused me to have an attitude adjustment!

So, what do I mean when I say attitude adjustment? This sermon changed my prayer! Praying the Word is one thing, but believing that God's promises are yea and amen is another. In due time, we will see the full manifestation of His promises come to pass at the appointed time, yielding a harvest of blessings.

We Must Watch Our Attitudes

As a believer, I know what to do after a good, old-fashioned prayer with the Lord. I know I am to pray in faith, believing that I have the petitions of my heart; to thank God for hearing my prayer; to wait patiently for God to manifest the answer, and to maintain a great posture of attitude. Well, I would love to tell you this has been my consistent and undying response between the promise and the blessing, but that would be less than the truth.

Prayer is a wonderful honor that God has allowed us to use to communicate our thanks, praise, and requests to Him. Prayer is comely and is our weapon of spiritual warfare that destroys yokes. There is an expectation that we have of God when we pray, just as God has expectations for us too. As prayer warriors, we expect God to lean in, take a seat, and bend His ear to our every whisper. We expect God will perform just like He did for the heroes of faith we read about in our Bibles.

You know, the ones to whom our God demonstrated His power and stretched out His mighty hand to deliver. They were the ones to whom God dispatched warring angels in order to conquer their enemies. The people whom God healed from certain deadly diseases, the women to whom God miraculously opened their wombs to bring forth life, or the men to whom God promised certain victory in battle.

When we pray as believers God expects some things from us too. God expects us to take Him at His Word, to have complete and unwavering faith, to not just wait impatiently but to wait with expectancy, to keep busy doing the Lord's work and not just sit idly by. He wants us to keep a good testimony while we wait for God's promises to manifest in our lives and to keep complaining far from our lips despite the "waiting period."

There is a waiting period of promise that we have come to expect after prayer is lifted up to our God. Although God does and has answered immediate prayer requests, God promises to hear our prayers and answer them too.

The Word says,

> *"according to your faith be it done unto you."*
> ~Matthew 9:29

Our attitudes make the difference in how we wait for the blessings to come. Attitude is a firm way of thinking that affects our actions. Attitude is like a remote that controls us. The remote can serve as a switch that changes our thoughts, actions, feelings, and expectations from positive to negative and back again. This is why we must watch our attitudes because it's so easy to switch based on feelings when God wants us to be controlled by faith. There is often a waiting period between the promise and the blessing. So, how should we wait?

Let us look to God's Word for some great examples.

Hannah's Attitude of Great Patience and Prayer

Hannah was waiting on God completely for answered prayer.

> *"And she was in bitterness of soul, and prayed unto the LORD, and wept sore. And she vowed a vow, and said, O LORD of hosts, if thou wilt indeed look on the affliction of thine handmaid, and remember me, and not forget thine handmaid, but wilt give unto thine handmaid a*

> *man child, then I will give him unto the LORD all the days of his life, and there shall no razor come upon his head.*
>
> *Wherefore it came to pass, when the time was come about after Hannah had conceived, that she bare a son, and called his name Samuel, saying, Because I have asked him of the LORD."*
> ~I Samuel 1:10-11, 20

Hannah also made a vow to support her request. Her request sealed her prayer in faith. She trusted God wholeheartedly and with great expectation. Some times our faith is increased by additional commitment and surrender to God.

The Children of Israel's Attitude of Disobedience

> *"For the children of Israel walked forty years in the wilderness, till all the people that were men of war, which came out of Egypt, were consumed, because they obeyed not*

the voice of the LORD: unto whom the LORD sware that he would not shew them the land, which the LORD sware unto their fathers that he would give us, a land that floweth with milk and honey."
~Joshua 5:6

Zachariah and Elizabeth Trusted God for a Son

In the Gospel of Luke, Chapter 1, we saw the story of Zachariah and his wife. They were righteous before God and were very steadfast in their service to God.

Even though they were trusting God for the fruit of the womb, they didn't allow their situation to stop their ministerial assignment.

In verses 13-14, Zachariah had an angelic visitation that confirmed that they had been praying.

"But the angel said to him: "Do not be afraid, Zechariah; your prayer has been heard. Your wife Elizabeth

> *will bear you a son, and you are to call him John. He will be a joy and delight to you, and many will rejoice because of his birth."*
>
> *~Luke 1:13-14*

As we trust God for miracles, signs, and wonders, and it seems as though nothing is going to come to pass, be encouraged by this story. Zachariah and his wife were old, but we still see God's glory as He blessed them with a special son, John the Baptist, who came to prepare the way for our Savior, Jesus Christ, our Lord!

Paul and Silas Waited with a Good Attitude of Expectation

In Acts 16:25–27, Paul and Silas gave us an example of how to wait in verse 25. We see how Paul and Silas were persecuted and put in prison. In prison, they were not dejected! They didn't complain! They didn't feel defeated! They praised God instead.

Here's a question... When trouble knocks on your door, how easy is it for you to face the challenges and stay in faith? Do you look at the problem, or do you look at the Problem Solver?

Hannah prayed, believing that God would answer her prayer, so she sealed her faith with a vow to the Lord.

Zachariah and Elizabeth remained steadfast in their service to God while they trusted Him for a miracle. They didn't allow their circumstances to stop them from serving God.

Paul and Silas prayed and believed in God while in bondage; they kept the faith, prayed continually, and expected a move from God.

Some Promises To Stand On In Faith

> *"And this is the confidence that we have in him, that, if we ask any thing according to his will, he heareth us:"*
> *~I John 5:14*

> *"Trust in the LORD with all your heart, and do not lean on your own understanding. In all your ways acknowledge him, and he will make*

straight your path."
~Proverbs 3:5-6

"But as for me, I watch in hope for the LORD, I wait for God my Savior; my God will hear me."
~Micah 7:7

"He wants to lead us in truth and teach us His ways. He is faithful as the God of our salvation. We can trust in Him while we wait."
~Psalm 27:14

"Is anything too hard for the Lord? At the appointed time I will return to you, about this time next year, and Sarah shall have a son."
~Genesis 18:14

"For the vision is yet for an appointed time, but at the end it shall speak, and not lie: though it tarry, wait for it; because it will surely come, it will not tarry."

~Habakkuk 2:3

Chapter 7

The Assurance Of God's Timing Coming To Pass

"Have you ever heard a promise speak?
Well, you just have to listen.
It wasn't a dream deferred; it was a vision of promise.
Imagination is not the creator; neither is the false hope of man.
Yet, I wait for the promise guaranteed,
With all the confidence and unwavering faith
that will surely succeed.
The promise will speak to all of God's seed."
~Myra P.

Habakkuk was a man of God with such great passion for God's truth. Some might say he was borderline disrespectful when demanding God answer him. Even the name Habakkuk means "to cling," so Habakkuk had no intention of letting go without an answer.

See, Habakkuk poured out his complaints to God, and like most of us, he was waiting impatiently for a response. He began to question God's timing because he felt God wasn't hearing or answering him fast enough. Sound familiar?

God tells Habakkuk,

> "Behold, ye among the heathen, and regard, and wonder marvelously: for I will work a work in your days which ye will not believe, though it be told you."
> ~Habakkuk 1:5

See, here is the promise God made to Habakkuk. Habakkuk proceeds to do something common among man in that his prayer turns into a barrage of questions.

The Assurance of God's Timing Coming To Pass

Sometimes when we communicate with God, we go from request to faith, then from questions to complaints.

> *"Thou art of purer eyes than to behold evil, and canst not look on iniquity: wherefore lookest thou upon them that deal treacherously, and holdest thy tongue when the wicked devoureth the man that is more righteous than he? And makest men as the fishes of the sea, as the creeping things, that have no ruler over them?"*
> *~Habakkuk 1:13-14*

In other words, Lord, you know how evil the wicked are! So, why do you let them live and not rebuke them?

> *"Therefore, they sacrifice unto their net, and burn incense unto their drag; because by them their portion is fat, and their meat plenteous. Shall they therefore empty their net, and not spare continually to slay the nations?"*
> *~Habakkuk 1:16-17 KJV*

Simply put, how long will you allow them to continue to have plenty to eat while they murder the people in your sight before you stop them?

Now the assurance comes in Chapter 2 as God answers him.

> "For the vision is yet for an appointed time, but at the end it shall speak, and not lie: though it tarry, wait for it; because it will surely come, it will not tarry.
>
> Behold, his soul which is lifted up is not upright in him: but the just shall live by his faith."
> ~Habakkuk 2:2-4

In other words, at the appointed time or Kairos time, I will do what I said I would do, but for now, write down what I show you. I guarantee it will happen! The righteous ones shall live because of their faith, so be patient.

I love this chapter in Habakkuk because it demonstrates God's assurance of His promises coming to pass at His divinely appointed moment. What a mighty God we serve!

The Promise Keeper

If you have ever had a promise broken, then you know how disappointed it can make you feel. The level of disappointment can vary depending on who broke the promise and what role the person plays in your life. A trusted friend, parent, spouse, co-worker, or even a child can be a source of great displeasure, hurt, or pain.

Today, few people value their "word as their bond" and have no qualms about breaking their promises. God is so concerned with keeping promises that He speaks extensively on the subject.

Here are some examples:

> *"But let your communication be, Yea, yea; Nay, nay: for whatsoever is more than these cometh of evil."*
> *Matthew 5:37*

> *"If a man vows a vow unto the*

LORD, or swear an oath to bind his soul with a bond; he shall not break his word, he shall do according to all that proceedeth out of his mouth."

Numbers 30:2

"God is not a man, that he should lie; neither the son of man, that he should repent: hath he said, and shall he not do it? or hath he spoken, and shall he not make it good?"

Numbers 23:19

"The Lord is not slack concerning his promise, as some men count slackness; but is longsuffering to usward, not willing that any should perish, but that all should come to repentance."

2 Peter 3:9

"My covenant will I not break, nor alter the thing that is gone out of my lips."

Psalm 89:34

God is our Promise Keeper! When God speaks, He breathes life. Isaiah 55:11 states,

> "So shall my word be that goeth forth out of my mouth: it shall not return unto me void, but it shall accomplish that which I please, and it shall prosper in the thing whereto I sent it".

That is why God's timing is so on-point, precise, exact, and on time. So, it behooves us as believers to be patient, have faith, and wait on the Lord. Man disappoints but God is sincere. Romans 3:4c-d says,

> *"let God be true, but every man a liar".*

Our faith, like Habakkuk's, will be tested. But God is so merciful to us because He has given us His Holy written testimony to encourage us daily. So, when we fall weak, we can find renewed strength as we wait on God's appointed time; for surely it shall come to pass!

"Take, my brethren, the prophets, who have spoken in the name of the Lord, for an example of suffering affliction, and of patience. Behold, we count them happy which endure. Ye have heard of the patience of Job, and have seen the end of the Lord; that the Lord is very pitiful, and of tender mercy."

James 5:10-11

Chapter 8
The Timing Of This Book, Why Now

The expression of a soul is the outpouring of a spiritual journey. This book is birthed out of my spiritual journey. Any author knows that writing is very personal and can leave you feeling very vulnerable. The words expressed reveal my inner most thoughts and feelings that I hope others will relate to and/or find a solace in.

For this book, I surrendered my time to God's timing and will. I say this because the experiences that life has given me have prepared me for such a time as this. There are so many things I am waiting on God for in my life. Waiting is never easy or pleasant in and of itself, but what makes it more difficult is when it seems as though you're watching everyone else pass you by at jet speed while you feel like you're sinking in quick sand. Having said this, I realize that perception can be shrouded in lies.

In other words, what you see is not always what you see! My grandmother used to say, "Everything that shines isn't gold." So, since we are not the authors and finishers of our lives, I am convinced we must seek the guidance of the One who is, Jesus Christ, Our Lord and Savior.

I am a Lady in Waiting. Some things I have waited so long for that I feel as though I can hardly breathe! Impatience tries to befriend me, but I consistently count him as an enemy. I have been a student of God's Word for years and am convinced that I must surrender and defer to the will of God for my life's journey.

What I have learned is:

- God knows more than I do.

- God sees and knows the end from the beginning.

- God is preparing me for the blessing before He gives it to me.

- My blessings have my name on them, M-Y- R-A!!!

- And they will undoubtedly locate me at the appointed time.

When I look back over my life, experience has reminded me that God is faithful, as promised. The blessings I have been given have been right on time, so what makes me think that God missed the express train to my house? He hasn't, nor will He ever!

Hum... *Don't you just love Him!*

Chapter 9
Waiting On God Is A Ministry! Practical Applications

Practical applications are like goody bags you can use to carry your leftovers home after you leave a restaurant. Yum! So, what can we place in our spiritual goody bags that we can carry with us? Some of these suggestions are recaps from this book, while others are newly mentioned suggestions.

1. Waiting on God is a Ministry

We are servants of the Most-High God therefore, we work for Him!

"If they obey and serve him, they

will spend the rest of their days in prosperity and their years in contentment."

~Job 36:11

Tip: Give God space to work in your life as He works His divine purpose in you.

_____
_____
_____
_____
_____
_____

2. Our Posture Matters

How we wait on God will determine our outcome. Practice an excellent attitude by waiting on God's Kairos timing. This can involve praises, prayers, faith, self-care, gratitude, serving others, fellowshipping, and on and on.

> *"Be joyful in hope, patient in affliction, faithful in prayer"*
> *~Romans 12:12*

Tip: God's timing is perfect in all things and in all ways.

_____
_____
_____
_____
_____
_____

3. Let Your Experiences Shape Your Expectations

There is nothing more satisfying than to know that if God did it before He will do it again. AMEN SOMEBODY!

> *"But ye are to hold fast to the Lord your God, as you have until now."*
> *~Joshua 23:8 KJV*

Tip: Let your expectations and experiences in Christ increase your faith.

_____
_____
_____
_____
_____
_____
_____

4. Let Go and Let God.

This may not be easy, but it's necessary. Don't put the cart before the horse. If you do, you will only delay your destiny, blessings, and timing.

> *"Be still before the Lord and wait patiently for him."*
> ~*Psalm 37:7*

Tip: God has already given you everything before you were born. He will give you what you need as you are ready and able to receive those needs.

_____

_____

_____

_____

_____

_____

5. Delay Is Not Denial.

Let's face it! No one really likes to wait for any reason. Some things take longer to happen than others.

> *"Do not be afraid, Daniel. Since the first day that you set your mind to gain understanding and to humble yourself before your God, your words were heard, and I have come in response to them."*
>
> *~Daniel 10:12*

Tip: Don't measure the length of time passed in order to determine the delivery of your desires.

_____
_____
_____
_____
_____
_____
_____

6. **Waiting Is Not A Punishment From God!**

Yes, sometimes we can delay our blessings by being disobedient; however, God is following the pattern that He planned for us from the beginning of time. This includes, yes, all the delays, even the ones we cause ourselves.

> *"For I know the plans I have for you," declares the Lord, "plans to prosper you and not to harm you, plans to give you hope and a future."*
> *~ Jeremiah 29:11*

Tip: Rest in the Lord and wait patiently for

Him to move as He sees fit.

Notes

Bibliography

[1] John Barr, From "Chronos" to "Kairos"- Responding to God's Appointed Time, 2014. https://www.weppinguca.org.

[2] Sarah Kessler, *Who's Father Time? Origins & Personification Explained*, 2021. https://www.joincake.com/blog/father-time.

[3] "Duration," Dictionary.com, https://www.dictionary.com/dictionary/duration.

[4] Loren Pinilis, *A Biblical View of Time: Shifting From Chronos to Kairos*, 2011.

Acknowledgments

To my beloved sons, Nigel and Michael: I thank my God every day for you! You make me smile and very proud. You are better than a thousand daughters! I love you very much!

To my two daughters-in-law, Kisha and Cora: I thank God for you as well. I know I raised my sons right when I see the families they created by choosing you as great and loving wives and mothers. I am a proud mother-in-law. My love for you has done nothing but grow over the years. Thank you both for all you do!

To my precious grandchildren: Orlando, Christina, and Marisa. I love you twice. Once because you are my children's children, and second, because you are special just because of who you are. I thank God for each of you carrying on our bloodline. I pray you always give God the Glory for all your blessings, knowing that grandma is praying for you!

XOXOXO

About The Author

Myra K. Pritchett was born in Brooklyn, New York, and raised in the Bronx, New York, by a father who was a United States Veteran and a mother who was an Elementary School Teacher, and in whose career path she followed.

Myra has earned a Masters in Special Education from the College of New Rochelle, a Masters in Christian Education from Hugee Theological Seminary, and a Doctorate in Ministry from Andersonville Theological Seminary.

Dr. Pritchett also holds an Evangelism certificate from the Hugee Theological Institute and is working on a certificate in Biblical Exposition in Greek and Hebrew.

A retired Elementary School Teacher after

29 years of dedicated service, she has taught General, Special Needs Children, and Adult Education. Myra Pritchett was Ordained as a Reverend on November 21, 2021 and is currently a Servant Leader at Mt. Lebanon Baptist Church in Peekskill, New York, where she enjoys evangelizing and teaching the Word of God through workshops and seminars.

At present, Dr. Pritchett is single, the proud mother of two sons, and a proud grandmother of three grandchildren.

Myra is a staunch supporter of empowering women to be all they can be in Christ. She is an educational advocate in leading by example and showing the importance of education.

Myra is a firm believer that "education is great but at the end of the day it shows you how much you really have left to learn, so remain humble as you climb the ladder of success."

Her motto is: Don't Give Up. "I can do all things through Christ which strengtheneth me," Philippians 4:13 KJV

www.ingramcontent.com/pod-product-compliance
Lightning Source LLC
Chambersburg PA
CBHW070047100426
42734CB00039B/2113